D0733841

ADIRONDACK
GHOSTS
II

ADIRONDACK GHOSTS II

Copyright © 2003 by Lynda Lee Macken. Printed and bound in the United States of America. All rights reserved. No part of this book may be reproduced or transmitted electronically, orally, or in any other fashion without permission in writing from the publisher. For information, please contact Black Cat Press, P. O. Box 1218, Forked River, NJ 08731-1218.

Although the author and publisher have made every effort to ensure the accuracy and completeness of information contained in this book, we assume no responsibility for errors, inaccuracies, omissions, or any inconsistency herein. Any slights of people, places, or organizations are unintentional.

ISBN 0-9700718-6-8

All photos by author.

Tratelja logo courtesy of Bolton Historical Society

Cover design by: Debra Tremper
                 Six Penny Graphics
                 Fredericksburg, VA

Back cover cat logo designed by: Glenda Moore
                                 catStuff Graphics

Printed on recycled paper by Sheridan Books. ♻

DEDICATION

To my parents who took me camping to the
Adirondacks when I was four years old.
My heart has never left.

The imposing Sagamore Resort is a popular Adirondack haunt.

CONTENTS

INTRODUCTION

On my first visit to Big Moose Lake, the last thing I expected to see was a ghost. I felt uneasy during my stay at Covewood Lodge and the reason became clear when a ribbon of mist floating over the lake took on the shape of a woman. I knew I was looking at a ghost.

Browsing in the main lodge the next day, a newspaper article reported the 1906 drowning of Grace Brown in Punky Bay - *the area from where the ethereal mist originated the night before.* The ghost now had a name.

Unsolved Mysteries recreated the sighting and told the story of the young woman's murder at the hand of Chester Gillette who was convicted and executed. The episode premiered in 1996 and can still be seen in re-run. The full account appears in *Adirondack Ghosts.*

I didn't know it at the time, but from that moment on my life changed. My enduring fascination with the spirit world combined with history and I embarked on a new career chronicling ghost stories.

The first printing of *Adirondack Ghosts* sold out in four months and has sold over 10,000 copies. Due to popular demand, I present to you *Adirondack Ghosts II.*

For the most part, Adirondack ghosts are like the mountain people themselves. They are friendly, some are helpful, and a number possess a great sense of humor. A few are somber and sad and continue a post mortem mourn. Many of them made indelible marks on the region like Abanakee Indian Sabael Benedict, ranger Major Robert Rogers, banker F. William Wait, and businessman Moses Cohen.

One of a kind characters found their way to the North Country. Melvil Dewey and Paul Smith, two genial hosts, early on catered to the tourist trade and ended up making fortunes. In addition to the legacies they left behind, the spirits of their wives apparently were so attached to their Adirondack abodes that they lingered long after they passed.

These are the spooky sagas of Adirondack spirits - lumberjacks, miners, and just plain folks who lived simple lives and stay behind haunting this storied land.

The author and UNSOLVED MYSTERIES producer, Jim Lindsay.

ADIRONDAC

For twenty years David Henderson had been in charge of Archibald McIntyre's iron mine. Problems loomed on the horizon for the iron works, so in 1845, Henderson went into the woods to search for a water source that would generate more power.

After several hours, he and his crew came upon a small pond swimming with ducks. Henderson handed over his pistol to John Cheney because he felt the guide was a better shot. Cheney aimed, but the ducks were spooked and flew out of range. The guide gave the gun back to its owner who tucked it away in its holster.

Cheney went to catch some fish while the others set up camp. No sooner had he made his first cast than he heard a pistol shot. When Cheney saw Henderson doubled over in pain, he was sickened to realize he had left the gun cocked. Henderson quickly died in the wilderness at the place now branded Calamity Pond.

The mining company declined and eventually went out of business in 1858. People rapidly left the hamlet - some left their furniture behind; they couldn't afford to move what little they had.

About a decade later, a New York businessman was vacationing in the mountains when he happened upon the deserted village of Adirondac. He entered one house and found it perfectly intact. A little further down the road the office of the mining company remained untouched - ledgers still sat open on the desk.

The businessman was fascinated with the ghost town and stayed longer than he had anticipated. Darkness was approaching and he needed to find a place to sleep - he had his choice of lodging in the empty town, so he chose the neatly furnished house, crawled under the covers and fell asleep.

In the middle of the night his sleep was disturbed by the sound of footsteps. Standing in the doorway was a male ghost who began to speak.

The phantom explained that he was the founder of the village and had a daughter named Mina. Mina had fallen in love with a young man who was an artist. The father didn't approve and sent the young man packing. The young couple started to correspond with each other, but the father intercepted the artist's letter to his daughter and concealed the note in a secure spot.

Soon after, Mina became seriously ill. The father searched in vain for her lover's letter but before he could find it, the young woman succumbed to her illness.

The father died shortly thereafter.

Now, he said, he was doomed to walk the earth until he found the letter. With that, the ghost vanished.

The sad story struck a chord with the visitor and he searched the house for hours. At last he reached into a hole in the wall and discovered the missing missive under a bird's nest. The businessman left the letter in full view on the kitchen table.

Content with his accommodations, the visitor stayed another night. This night he heard the restless spirit's cry of joy upon spotting the unearthed note. The elated father was finally freed from his eternal unrest.

ALDER CREEK

Louis C. Jones, Ph.D. was one of the first to investigate the supernatural in the Empire State. As Director of the New York State Historical Society, he was an outstanding authority on ghost lore.

In *Things That Go Bump in The Night*, Dr. Jones described a house on the state road in Alder Creek, torn down twenty years ago, where the front window was in constant need of boarding up. Every time a new glass was installed, the panes shattered as night fell.

There was no explanation for this phenomenon until someone remembered that a raucous party had taken place in the house. During the festivities a young man had been thrown through the window to his death.

Were the broken panes his way of showing his resentment from beyond the grave or was this pesky behavior a message of warning to would-be revelers?

GHOST BRIDGE

One of the country's oldest tourist attractions is Ausable Chasm, the Grand Canyon of the North East.

William Gilliland of County Armagh, Ireland, is credited with discovering the natural wonder in 1765.

In 1793, the first of many bridges to span Ausable Chasm was called High Bridge. Huge Norway pines were laid from bank to bank across the divide and six stringers, each about twenty inches wide, supported a roadway constructed of heavy cross planks.

Freak storms have always wrecked havoc with bridges over the gorge, and as recently as 1996, rainstorms dumped torrents of water that tore steel bridges from their foundations and sent them crashing down the cliffs.

Such was the case long before Ausable Chasm was a tourist stop. A wooden bridge that spanned the gorge was wiped out; all that remained was one stringer, an 18-inch square beam.

The bridge was never rebuilt; instead traffic was re-routed to Ausable Forks. The single wooden girder remained across the chasm and was left in place.

One stormy night, years later, a stranger entered an Ausable Forks tavern. He was soaking wet, but quickly dried off and dug into his hot meal. The innkeeper struck up a conversation with the newcomer.

"Terrible night to be out," he began.

The stranger agreed and went on to say that he knew the area well as he had lived in the town 20 years ago and was glad that the old wooden bridge was still intact. He added that he had helped to construct the darn thing.

His statement caught the attention of everyone in the tavern and they chimed in that the bridge had been washed out years ago.

The stranger kept on chewing and calmly declared that he had driven across the bridge. He heard the horse's hooves on the wooden planks and the rushing water as it crashed 125 feet down into the canyon.

An argument broke out and the stranger made bets that the bridge was still standing.

The next morning practically the entire town showed up at the site of the old bridge. They plainly saw the horse's hoof prints from the night before; they led from the girder across the gorge and up to the tavern. A young daredevil walked across the narrow beam and sure enough there was a similar trail on the other side.

The story doesn't end there for when the stranger realized that only a single strut crossed the precipice, his hair instantly turned from jet black to snow white and he started to shake uncontrollably. The "shakes" stayed with him for the rest of his life.

MARANVILLE FARM

Bolton Landing evolved from an Indian campground along a wilderness trail to an enclave for America's rich and famous who built their summer estates on the rim of Lake George. The mansions, stables and boathouses that lined the shoreline in the late 1800s gave this area the nickname "Millionaire's Row."

In 1886, James Lincoln Maranville operated a stage and cargo line from the steamer landing in Bolton to the railroad station at Lake George and back. The stagecoach stop was located behind the Mountaineer Inn, today's Frederick's restaurant.

The Maranville homestead sits high in the hills over Bolton Landing and was once the headquarters for the stagecoach line.

If the Maranville name rings a bell, their service station in town was a natural occupational shift when in the 1920s "horsepower" took on a whole new meaning. At first, the station pumped three brands of gas, Sunoco, Mobil, and Esso – a common practice at the time.

In addition to pumping gas and repairing cars, Owen Kilburn (O.K.) Maranville operated a taxi business in the 1920s and 30s and augmented his income by chauffeuring the affluent from Canada to Florida.

The station still sells gas *and* repairs cars - a vanishing combination.

In the 1950s when the market for junk parts declined, James Baird Maranville dug a huge pit across from his house and buried his jalopies in a mass grave.

Under the circumstances, it's no surprise that when the family received visitors from the other side, they pulled into the Maranville's driveway in a supernatural automobile.

Often, and at any time of day or night, the crunch of gravel was heard as a ghost car pulled onto the property and the slam of car doors was audible as the phantom passengers disembarked. The invisible vehicle and its intangible occupants baffled the inhabitants of the house.

Maranville family members, with their characteristic good humor, could only conjure up one explanation. They thought it probable that the spectral auto was the spirit of one of the many buried across the street.

MAYFAIR RESORT

Let me start off by saying that the Mayfair Resort is *not* haunted, but the spirit of a sweet and gentle cat named Mooey lingered briefly for a last goodbye.

Nowadays, summer visitors lodge at motels along Lakeshore Drive, the ten-mile stretch of road between Lake George and Bolton Landing. These hostelries stand on sites where elegant mansions once stood. For almost a hundred years, the road itself was known as "Millionaire's Row."

The Golden Age of Millionaires Row started shortly after the Civil War and extended into the 1950s. During World War I, Dr. William Gerard Beckers made millions when he revolutionized American dye making. He created the most opulent estate of them all - Villa Marie Antoinette.

Beckers constructed his 40-room castle overlooking Huddle Bay. Artisans from Europe carved fireplaces, painted murals, and decorated walls and ceilings with gold leaf. The floors were Italian marble, bathroom fixtures were solid gold, and the dining room was paneled with Wedgwood porcelain.

By 1953, the era of Millionaire's Row was coming to a close. New owners found the Villa impractical. They did explore the possibility of maintaining the manse as a museum but costs were prohibitive. The contents were sold at auction.

The Mayfair Resort was built on property that was once part of Beckers' 90-acre estate.

For twenty years the Mayfair has been my home away from home and my friendship with the owners, Mary and George Baer, and their cats, makes my stays memorable.

Their friendly felines greet me upon every arrival, and until she passed away, Mooey kept me company by staying in my room overnight. Her favorite perch was the pillow on the empty adjacent bed.

My heart was broken when I learned of Mooey's death and my first trip to the Mayfair without her was heart wrenching. I missed my furry friend terribly and struggled with my tears.

That first night, as I prepared to settle down to sleep, I looked over at the empty bed and saw a definite indentation on the pillow in Mooey's usual spot. My dearly departed friend *was* there, only now in spirit form.

Mooey Cat made a post-mortem visit to comfort a friend.

RECLUSE ISLAND

Lake George is dotted with almost two hundred islands, some with intriguing names such as Hermit Island, Gem Island, As You Were Island, Recluse Island, and Phantom Island. No one knows for sure if a ghost inhabited Phantom Island - maybe the atoll appeared ghostly when shrouded in fog or early morning mist.

Recluse Island is the one that is reputedly haunted. The island received its name because a Jesuit priest lived a solitary life on the tiny isle. Recluse, located just east of the Algonquin Restaurant and Chic's Marina, was the first to have a permanent residence.

Supreme Court Justice Pliny Saxton built a colonial style home on Recluse in the late 19th century. When that structure burned down in 1914, a more elaborate edifice was erected as a wedding gift for the justice's granddaughter. Tragically, while vacationing in Europe, the young woman died. The grief stricken family wired home to sell the property. That's when the Reynolds family purchased the island, ghosts and all.

In 1942, the Reynolds' grandmother's dying wish was to have "one more summer" at the beautiful setting. It appears her wish has been granted.

According to an *Adirondack Life* article by Christopher Shaw, those who sense the matriarch's presence say it is strongest in her second floor bedroom. That is also the room where those who witnessed her apparition caught her staring at them from the mirror over the dresser.

The most startling manifestation of all was when the grandmother appeared to a four-year-old boy. He encountered her standing on the spiral staircase in her favorite purple dress; the affable woman beckoned him to follow her.

The Reynolds and their guests have experienced other bizarre events such as rattling doors, disembodied footsteps, and the full-bodied apparition of an 18th century soldier standing on the patio in full view. The confused colonial is probably a leftover from the French and Indian conflicts fought in the area.

Some visitors are unable to stay the night at the island dwelling. The ghostly energies are so unsettling that guests demand to be spirited away to the mainland.

Recluse Island is an intensely spirited spot.

Sagamore Resort's Club Grill is a favored spot for specters.

14

SAGAMORE RESORT

Bolton Landing is about 10 miles north of Lake George village and is home to about 2,000 people year round who enjoy one of the most scenic settings in all of the Adirondacks. From the town, the view of Lake George takes in the two tallest mountains that rise from the eastern shore, Black Mountain and Buck Mountain, along with Tongue Mountain to the north.

The lake's irregular shoreline here harbors a series of little coves and dozens of islands, including the largest - Green Island, home of the Sagamore Resort, one of the most famous resorts in the Adirondacks.

The present day Sagamore is the third hotel by that name constructed on the site. The first two were consumed by fire. Although no casualties were reported, one intuitive feels that the specter of a little girl who looks out over the lake from an eastern oriented window may be a revenant of one of the awful conflagrations.

The history of the Sagamore begins in 1881 when hotel operator Myron O. Brown sought the support of four Philadelphia millionaires to begin construction of an exclusive resort community on the 70-acre island. By the time the hotel opened its doors two years later a wooden bridge was in place connecting Green Island to the mainland.

The Victorian structure faced Lake George, providing fantastic views from the wraparound porch, and accommodated 300 guests offering a lake vista from every room.

Guests arrived and departed via steamboats that operated from Lake George Village since the stagecoach run through Bolton was limited in those days. (At the time, Bolton consisted of four homes, one store and the Baptist Church.)

After only ten years of operation a fire erupted in the laundry and the wooden edifice burned to the ground. The decision was made to rebuild immediately although insurance covered only half of the loss.

Re-opened in the summer of 1894, with Myron Brown still at the helm, the second Sagamore Hotel had the added amenities of private baths, elevators, tennis courts, stables, and a bowling alley for its 300 guests.

Twenty years later, on Easter Sunday, again fire ravished the hotel. Since the Sagamore was only opened seasonally for the summer, no one was killed.

The Sagamore was fully reconstructed in 1930 through the efforts of Dr. William G. Beckers of New York City, one of the hotel's early stockholders, and William H. Bixby, a St. Louis industrialist. Together they financed the cost despite the economic depression.

In 1985, after a $75 million restoration, the 350-room resort opened for a fourth time, and is proudly listed in the National Register of Historic Places.

Avid history buff and Sagamore security officer Jerry Bearden has worked for the hotel for 16 years. Bearden has heard some fantastic tales during his tenure.

Mister Brown's is the resort's Adirondack-styled eatery and a strange incident took place in the restaurant's kitchen one memorable morning.

Around 3:00 A.M. as the chef was straightening up, he was listening to rap music on the radio. A tall, female specter in a long white gown appeared before him. She pointed to the radio and asked, "Whose words are these?"

The cook was chilled to the bone as the phantom passed right through him; he watched in disbelief as she floated down the hall. The chef raced to the security office to tell his tale and appeared as "white as a sheet." He resigned on the spot.

The Trillium Restaurant offers "exquisite cuisine" and is a favorite dining spot for many guests but an ethereal pair like it best. Around closing, when things have quieted down for the night a ghostly couple dressed in vintage eveningwear descends the stairs and enters the dining room. Intuitives feel they are leftover from the earliest Sagamore structure.

The wraith of a little girl has been seen in The Veranda, a glass-enclosed room that affords a panoramic view of Lake George. Her late 19th century garb dates her to the first hotel as well.

In 1938, the Sagamore purchased the privately owned 18-hole golf course and club house built ten years earlier on the mainland's Federal Hill.

About fifty years ago, a local boy delighted in retrieving golf balls that had gone astray. He would take his finds to the pro shop and probably earned some good tips for his efforts. Tragically his life was cut short when a car accidentally ran over him.

Not to be deterred, the young man carries on his work from beyond the grave and is quite regularly seen on mist laden mornings ambling about the greens near the place where he perished.

It is quite possible that some ghosts from the resort's Green Island location frequent the country club's restaurant, the Club Grill. After hours an ethereal couple is momentarily seen in the dining room. A female specter with a blank stare has been spotted standing outside the screened-in porch.

A restaurant security guard thought he was dreaming when he saw the apparition of an elderly gent in a rocking chair.

When the clubhouse restaurant was being refurbished the imbedded spirits felt out of place; just about every employee caught glimpses of the restless spirits in their peripheral vision.

When photos were taken to embellish the resort's menus, some shots captured the ghostly image of a Victorian boy. How many diners have looked at the offerings on the breakfast menu and were oblivious to the phantom face of a long ago boy peering out at them?

The Sagamore's friendly spirits are known to play tricks. One baffling antic is that the keys that are locked in the key box are sometimes found with their chains knotted together. This is a mystery without explanation. Could it be ghosts?

TRATELJA

Stone ruins are all that remain of a once elegant manor house that stood in the hills over Bolton Landing.

In the early 1900s, Dr. Carl Jonas Nordstrom and his wife, Caroline Emily Brereton, opted to erect their large summer home on a mountaintop miles away from Millionaire's Row. Their 850-acre site commanded a magnificent view of Lake George.

They named their home *Tratelja* the Swedish word for "woodcutter."

Tratelja stood three stories high. The first level was constructed of natural uncut stone from the surrounding area and the top levels were stucco and wood.

Guests disembarked from carriages, and later automobiles, at the lovely portico off the semi-circular drive of the L-shaped dwelling.

Today the remains of an immense fireplace with three openings stand sentinel; this unique firebox could heat three rooms at one time. This was only one of many throughout the huge 30-room house.

A fountain, tiered garden, and goldfish pond decorated the rear of the house. The property also consisted of a caretaker's cottage, several outbuildings, a stone barn and two farms, East and West.

Tratelja's 35 employees operated the estate's sawmill and cared for 50 sheep, cows, ducks, horses, donkeys, and 1500 chickens. During the war years, the

Nordstroms had the sheep sheared and donated the wool to the American Red Cross. *Tratelja's* eggs were served in Glens Falls' restaurants

The soft-spoken Nordstrom was a mystery unto himself. Little is known about the man described as an easygoing, gentleman farmer. Some reports label him a Danish nobleman while others list him as a native of Sweden. He was never known to perform any medical services and census reports list no occupation.

Mrs. Nordstrom, who preferred to be called "Emily," was the sister of Senator H.E.H. Brereton of Bolton. She was active in the Women's Suffrage movement and gave many speeches on the subject in the area. Her husband was always present at these meetings to show his support. Those who knew Emily describe her as a charming, gentle woman.

Emily's compassionate side was shown when she opened her home to the elderly for a few months in 1922.

When Mrs. Nordstrom died in 1934, Carl simply abandoned *Tratelja*, furnishings and all. He passed away four years later in Clearwater, Florida where he is buried. Emily is interred in the family plot in Bolton Cemetery.

The Nordstrom's sister-in-law established a health clinic for the indigent in Glens Falls for those in need of social, medical and educational help.

Tratelja became a satellite center and was the perfect setting for those in need of a supervised living program and low cost psychotherapy. Dr. John A. P. Millet, whose father perished on the *Titanic*, was in charge of the operation. Many locals served as nurses, custodians, and volunteers.

Unfortunately, only three years later, fire destroyed the magnificent estate but all fifty patients were safely evacuated.

For years, the ghostly ruins inspired scary stories among local teens. These spooky tales are not without merit for indeed the property is reputedly home to a blond-haired spirit.

Her specter has been sighted inside the old farmhouse across the highway. At times she appears as a full-bodied apparition, and on one occasion, allegedly spoke to a houseguest and described herself as being eighteen years old.

A former owner frequently spied the young specter in her peripheral vision and often experienced cupboard doors opening and closing as if the entity was going about the house as she did in life.

A light in the stone barn oftentimes bedeviled the residents. Seeing a glow, they would rush to the stables afraid it was fire. When they opened the doors they found only darkness.

TRATELJA

21

"Emma" is a friendly spirit still attached to Landon Hill B & B.

LANDON HILL B&B

In 1862, Landon Hill B&B was originally built as a dream home for a Philadelphia bride. The lumber baron's home in the hamlet of Chestertown was constructed on a hilltop overlooking the comings and goings of the town at the crossroads of Routes 8 and 9.

The distinguished manse was initially adorned with a wraparound porch and encrusted with gingerbread.

Landon Hill Road was a short cut onto Route 8 and during prohibition the thoroughfare was known as "Rum Runners' Alley." A number of slot machines were found in the house so it is surmised that the residence was once a casino and most likely a gin joint.

Clearly the house has a long and colorful history and its haunted reputation goes back decades.

At first the property was a working farm complete with horse barns, carriage house, and various outbuildings to support the homestead; the house saw incarnations as an apartment house, sanitarium for tuberculosis sufferers, and an American Legion Post. Some believe the red light that used to be seen in the window signaled that the bordello was up and running.

A retired schoolteacher resided in one of the apartments and over the years shared with *everyone* of her students the stories of her experiences with the ghost at the Landon Hill house.

The rooms of her apartment were once the servants' quarters. The educator claimed that the ghost, affectionally known as "Emma," never let her sleep - the spirit constantly pulled off the bedcovers.

Judy and Carl Johnson purchased the property in 1995 and immediately sensed that they were not alone.

Once an extremely heavy mirror fell off the wall. Well, not exactly. What they witnessed looked as if someone *lifted* the glass off the wall and then gently *rocked* the heavy piece across the room.

At one time their daughter-in-law heard the door of the Sunset Room slam shut and then she discerned sobbing emanating from the room.

Sometimes when Judy is cleaning upstairs she hears the indistinct sound of voices.

Electrical anomalies are commonly experienced. Radios, TVs, lamps, stereos all come on from time to time *even when they are not plugged in.* This is one powerful ghost.

But to tell the truth, the life force inside the historic home is rarely obnoxious. The Johnson's find their invisible tenant to be quite helpful especially when it comes to finding lost objects. The spirit exudes a soothing and peaceful energy and the couple feels protected by its presence.

F. W. WAIT HOUSE

Nicknamed "Hometown U.S.A." by *Look* magazine, the moniker still fits. In fact, *Reader's Digest* named Glens Falls the "16th best place to raise a family in America."

Abraham Wing, named the community Wing's Falls, when he settled the area in 1763, but the name was changed to Glen's Falls when Abe lost a card game to Colonel Johannes Glen.

In 1851, the Cushing family built a brick Federal style home on Warren Street that today is occupied by the offices of Planned Parenthood. 150 years ago, the house was a stop on the Underground Railroad and the "hidey holes" in the cellar exude such an eerie feeling that some staffers refuse to go down there alone.

F. William Wait was a successful banker who moved his family into the Cushing home. Whenever William was away on business an invisible presence sat in the living room rocking in a rocking chair. The moment William arrived home, the rocking stopped. According to Pitkin in *Ghosts of the Northeast*, this happened *every* time William was away until the family renovated the home, which probably confounded the spirit.

Now that the women's social service agency occupies the house, the spirit has made a comeback. Sometimes the apparition of a Victorian woman dressed in a long black skirt and white high-collared blouse with a brooch at the neck shows up in the kitchenette.

Phantoms inside St. Mary's Church figure prominently in an old Irish legend.

ST. MARY'S CHURCH

According to an old Irish legend, deceased priests have long been known to continue saying mass in their parishes long after they've left the mortal world.

In *Things That Go Bump in The Night* by Louis C. Jones, this happened in St. Mary's Church at the stroke of midnight and was witnessed by a man who had fallen asleep in a rear pew.

Another ghostly oddity at the church concerns a man coming home from work one night. As he walked by St. Mary's he saw lights on inside and heard enthusiastic singing. He wondered what was going on but as he tried to enter the church he found that the door was locked.

This is strange, he thought, so he shimmied up an outside wall and peered through a window. He recognized the priest and everyone inside; all were former friends and neighbors and *all of them had been long dead and buried!*

SABAEL

The town of Indian Lake is indirectly named for its first settler, Sabael Benedict, a member of the Abanakee Indian tribe from Canada.

In order to avoid fighting against the United States in the French and Indian War, Sabael left his tribe in 1762, thereby relinquishing his yearly stipend, set off through the wilderness, and settled on the lonely lake. At that time the country was well stocked with moose, beaver, otter, and deer.

Indian Lake remained largely undiscovered until the Adirondack Railroad, linking Saratoga Springs to North Creek, was built in 1871. This brought wealthy vacationers within twenty miles of Indian Lake, and many began to venture to the town via horse-drawn buckboard wagons, then farther into the beauty of its surrounding wilderness with professional guides.

For weeks on end, Sabael would take his canoe, gun and traps, and go off alone hunting. He admitted that he was never afraid when he was alone, except sometimes he was frightened of "Chepi" (ghosts).

Sabael raised one son and three daughters whose descendents are still citizens of the hamlet. The family's dirt floor wigwam was furnished with a few deerskins, and the usual eating and cooking utensils. The simple home held no table, chair, or bed; their custom was to sit, eat, and sleep on the bare ground year round.

Sabael claimed that he was the first to discover the iron mine at Keeseville, and sold the knowledge of it to a white man for a bushel of corn, and a dollar in money.

He spoke some English, was Catholic, and carried a string of rosary beads, which a priest gave him, and felt they possessed great power: *"Spose me out on lake, wind blow hard, lake all too high for canoe; me drop one bead into lake, all calm and still in moment. Spose me in woods, thunder bang strike tree, me 'fraid; hang these upon limb of tree, thunder all go 'way, no hurt me. Spose woods full of Chepi, take these beads out, all Chepi run 'way."*

After Sabael passed, a ghostly legend grew around his gentle spirit. The story goes that one day Sabael left his home and went off into the woods on one of his usual forays. Day turned into night and his wife's wait turned into worry. She went off onto the frozen expanse of Indian Lake to look for Sabael, but her search was in vain.

Her frozen body was found a few days later; ultimately her remains were buried on a small island in the lake.

Legend says that on cold winter nights, if you listen closely, you can still hear Sabael calling out for his wife.

The former Dunn House - home to many lost souls.

DUNN HOUSE

In 1840, John and Catherine Dunn constructed a 2½-story Federal style home in Johnsburg. Their lavish estate had verdant lawns, burgeoning flowerbeds, a greenhouse, and carriage house, horse barns, guesthouses and servants' quarters, all hallmarks of Dunn's success.

But after the patriarch died, the family fell on hard times. Two sisters, Catherine and Margaret, barely managed to maintain the home; they died in 1878 and 1893 respectively. Their mortal remains may be buried in the graveyard across the street but psychics say their spirits remain in the home they treasured.

Over the next 100 years, a number of families and entrepreneurs tried to make a go of the place. At the turn of the 20th century, summer tourists knew the spot as "The Adirondack Inn." After World War II, the property operated as a girl's camp.

In 1953, Mt. Crane Lodge opened and stayed in business until the owner's wife shot herself. She was found dead in her car on a lonely road in the next town.

For years, passers by reported seeing a female apparition in Victorian era dress standing in front of an attic window and waving. Most likely this is the same phantom who streaked across the road from the cemetery and caught the attention of the present owner who ended up purchasing the house fifteen years later.

With the owners' blessing, author David J. Pitkin assembled a team of clairvoyants, who had no prior knowledge of its history, to explore the house. Their impressions were startling and confirmed the couple's suspicions that they were living in a haunted house.

In earlier days, the attic was the domain of the hired help. The intuitives picked up on the presence of a ghostly girl hiding in the upper room and a laborer carrying out his mortal tasks in the afterlife.

They glimpsed a woman in black anxiously pacing back and forth in one of the small bedrooms. After processing the information with the owners, they determined that this specter was most likely Margaret who had sold the house and was allowed to stay in an attic room only out of kindness from the new owners.

Margaret worried that one day she would be forced out of the home she loved, but when she died of arteriosclerosis, she wasn't aware of her own passing.

Nor does she recognize Catherine's spirit who also lingers here. Since Catherine was the more social of the two sisters, she is probably the woman who waves to the outside world.

Others spiritual remnants in the house include a woman who hung herself in an attached shed and the husband of the wife who committed suicide. His spirit remains in the basement teary-faced and sitting with a bottle of alcohol that he used to drown his sorrows.

The present owners' desire is to restore the historic house to its former grandeur. On a higher level, they wish to spiritually cleanse the environment of its troubled spirits, eliminate the sadness emanating from the failed souls, and help them move on to a place of greater peace.

MILL CREEK

In 1896, according to Frederick C. Aber Jr. in *Adirondack Folks*, a young man reported that he had seen the apparition of a ghost floating just below the falls in the town of Johnsburg.

Later that year, four different people observed strange lights in that same location.

Over the years, many others driving by and walking along the creek were astonished when they witnessed the unknown specter.

The townsfolk could only conclude that there was no explanation for the eerie sightings other than a ghost.

LAKE CHAMPLAIN

French Canadian storyteller Catherine LaBier grew up in Whitehall and specializes in recounting ghostly tales that revolve around family life and reveal a message. Like the one about...

...Marie Josette who lived with her family near a swampy area of Lake Champlain.

Her mother was planning a party and was involved in all its preparations. Marie had plans too - to run away with a boy that she loved.

Mother and daughter fought over this idea, but as night was falling, Marie slipped away to meet her intended.

The lights of the rising swamp gases, called "feu follet," illuminated a path through the marshland. Marie believed that the glowing orbs were signals from her sweetheart. She followed the lights into deeper and deeper water until she eventually drowned.

Her mother was inconsolable when she learned of her daughter's death especially since they had parted on such bad terms. Exactly one year later the mother died.

Legend says that on the anniversary of the two deaths, people fishing in that area of the lake hear dishes rattling and laughter coming from the deserted family home. They say the happy sounds are the mother and the daughter who made amends and reunited in heaven.

A ghostly fish story is another haunting tale to come out of Lake Champlain.

One foggy afternoon a New Jersey fisherman was excited to hear that bullheads were biting in the lake. He grabbed his rod and tackle and hiked two miles to the boathouse. Unfortunately, by the time he arrived all the boats were out.

As the disappointed angler started to drag himself back to his lodging, a motorboat pulled up to the shoreline and a young man shouted, "Hey mister, why you looking so glum?"

The Jersey man explained that he was eager to fish but couldn't get a boat. The boy offered to take him out for a few hours and the fisherman took the bait.

The fishing was great until it started to drizzle and the sky grew dark with storm clouds. The man sat for an hour without a nibble and finally asked the boy to take him back to shore.

As soon as they were underway, the boy turned the boat in the opposite direction and shouted over his shoulder that he just wanted to visit his mom for a minute - she lived on the other side of the lake.

The man said "sure," after all the boy was nice enough to afford him the pleasure of fishing.

The pair arrived at the dock and the boy asked the angler to wait in the boat; he'd only be a minute.

After a half an hour sitting out in the rain the man grew impatient and finally walked up to the house and knocked on the door.

An old woman answered and the man asked if the boy could come out and bring him back home.

"What boy?" she asked.

The man told her his story, how the young boy picked him up and took him fishing, then said he wanted to visit his mother.

The woman asked him to describe the boy.

The man was bewildered but described the youth as tall, about 5 ft. 10 in., maybe 185 pounds, and he was wearing a red and blue jacket.

The old lady fainted.

The fisherman picked her up and carried her to the couch where he revived her with a glass of cool water.

She asked him to tell her the story again.

"Look, if you don't believe me, I'll show you the boat at the landing," he said.

When they arrived at the landing *there was no boat.*

The woman led him back to the house and told him a story. It was just about a year ago that her son had left to go fishing out on Lake Champlain. His boat capsized and the young man drowned. Neither the boat nor his body were ever found.

LAKE GEORGE MUSEUM

In 1646, Jesuit missionary Father Isaac Jogues named the beautiful body of water we know as Lake George, Lac du Saint Sacrement, meaning "Lake of the Blessed Sacrement".

The lake was given its present name in 1755 by Sir William Johnson to honor King George II of England.

The 32-mile-long waterway is fed by underground springs and has more than a hundred miles of shoreline.

Lake George played a significant role in the birth of our nation. James Fenimore Cooper's classic tale *The Last of the Mohicans* was based on the battles in this region during the French and Indian War in the 1750s. In 1775, the north end of the lake at Fort Ticonderoga was the sight of the colonists' first victory in the American Revolution, as Ethan Allen and his Green Mountain Boys, together with Benedict Arnold, seized the fort from the British.

Robert Rogers was a crucial player in every major battle of the French and Indian War. A mountain on the west side of Lake George with an almost vertical rock wall commemorates his place in Adirondack history. The mountain is named Rogers Rock and the wall is called Rogers Slide.

Born in 1731 in Methuen, a small town in the Massachusetts Bay Colony, Rogers grew up amidst the worry of war. In 1744, France declared war against

Major Robert Rogers' infamous bird whistle calls pierce the peace and quiet of the Lake George Museum.

Great Britain and news quickly spread that the Indians had banded with the French and were launching barbaric and unpredictable assaults against homesteaders near Lake Champlain.

Young Rogers knew at an early age that he was not cut out for farming and marriage. He was a woodsman - an individual who loved hunting and learned early to survive in the wilderness. Rogers longed to know the world beyond his Bay Colony.

Massachusetts was seeking volunteers and Rogers saw an opportunity. He claimed that he could recruit scouts who could keep watch on the rivers, lakes and woodlands, and then report back their findings.

Starting mostly with men from New Hampshire, Rogers sought only those who were brave and with strong character. He ended up organizing and leading a formidable fighting force.

For twenty years, Rogers' Rangers, as they came to be known, used tactics learned from the Indians to harass, ambush and attack the enemy. His personal diary at the Fort Ticonderoga Museum lists missions conducted from his base of operations at Fort Edward, to all of the territory north of Lake George, and west to what is now Detroit, Michigan.

He writes of continuous hardships endured due to living in debt from lack of government support for his scouting activities.

This legendary frontiersman is best remembered for his daring exploit in 1758 when he escaped death by a characteristic dodge. Rogers and his men were outnumbered three to one; their strategy was every man for himself.

Rogers was being hotly pursued and when he came to a precipice overlooking Lake George. To most, the predicament meant certain death, but the legendary frontiersman would not be defeated. He undid his heavy pack and pushed it over the edge of the cliff; the pack left a track in its wake that resembled the fall of a human body. Then he strapped his snowshoes on backwards and made the descent to the frozen lake. Retrieving his pack he reversed his snowshoes and was off toward Fort William Henry.

When the Indians reached the edge they were stunned that they had been outmaneuvered and decided that the Great Spirit must protect Rogers. They gave up the chase.

Major Robert Rogers died in poverty in England in 1795 but he left behind a legacy of leadership that lives on in the United States Army Ranger Department.

Along with several other ghosts, Rogers' spirit lives on in the old Warren County courthouse that is home to the Lake George Historical Association. Quite regularly, his infamous bird whistle calls pierce the peace and quiet of the museum.

Visitors to the museum have shared that they have sighted spectral forms in the basement jail cells.

Museum workers offered two more puzzling phenomenon. Even though the radio is unplugged and without batteries it still plays music from time to time. When chairs that have been pushed in under the library table are pulled out, they have small puddles of water on the seats.

LAKE SHORE DRIVE

Even though Lake George Village is the commercial hub of the southern Adirondacks, the town has managed to stay virtually the same year after year. The lake's natural beauty remains as awe-inspiring as the day when Thomas Jefferson wrote to his daughter, "Lake George is without comparison, and the most beautiful water I ever saw."

Lake George's history is rooted in its role as an important outpost during the French and Indian Wars. Fort William Henry was the site of horrific battles in the 1750s, which inspired *The Last of the Mohicans.*

The original site of the fort was reconstructed in 1953, and now serves as one of the primary tourist attractions in the village.

According to storyteller Shirley McFerson, phantoms from the past routinely roam the village roads. Sometimes, soldiers dressed in 18th century uniforms, who appear to be re-enactors from Fort William Henry, are actually revenants from the war fought on the town's turf; their ghosts are trapped in another dimension.

Perhaps out of a sense of duty they stay behind looking to complete their earthly assignment.

The village of Lake George offers one of the prettiest waterfront walks in America - the nicely landscaped promenade displays fabulous views of the mountain-framed lake.

A spectral soldier disembarked from a ghostly train at the 1911 Delaware & Hudson station.

If you catch it just right, late in the day or at the crack of dawn before the boats and Jet Skis take over, you may glimpse a sight of sheer unnatural phenomenon that will stay with you for a long time.

Ms. McFerson timed it just right the day she and a friend were enjoying their brisk morning walk along Lake Shore Drive.

Everything seemed perfectly normal until the pair approached the old Delaware & Hudson train station (now home to a plethora of souvenir shops). Shirley noticed the atmosphere became still and all seemed strangely quiet. The gentle sounds of the water lapping and birds chirping suddenly ceased.

On the opposite side of the street, she spied what appeared to be a World War I soldier standing with his suitcase. Had he just disembarked from his train at the long ago station?

He surveyed his surroundings then started to walk toward Canada Street. Slowly he faded from view.

After the soldier passed the air again was abuzz with the usual morning activity.

Was this sighting a glimpse into another dimension? Was this young man from decades ago returning from war happy to be back? Perhaps he was a casualty longing to return to the place and people that he loved...

...We can only ponder spectral incidents and the purpose of those on the other side.

Some feel that the Fuller House shelters a reunited mother and daughter from the other side.

WIAWAKA

One hundred years ago, financier Spencer Trask, and his wife Katrina donated property and buildings on the eastern shore of Lake George as a retreat for self-supporting women from the shirt factories and textiles mills in Troy and Cohoes. The resort was named *Wiawaka,* a Native American word meaning "the spirit of God in woman."

The centerpiece of the affordable respite is the beautifully restored Second Empire style Fuller House, named after Katrina Trask's best friend and first director of the camp, Mary Fuller.

In the 1990s, staff members began to witness some odd goings on inside the impressive building. The cook saw a woman's lower legs and feet going up the back staircase. On another occasion all she saw was the disembodied feet walking up the stairs. Footsteps were also audible in the attic.

The sound of dishes rattling signal breakfast preparation but when the kitchen doors are opened no one is there. Who is the unseen helper? Many feel the ghost is Rachel, a young woman who froze to death in Waconda Lodge when the caretaker turned her away.

According to *Ghosts of the Northeast,* Rachel's mother worked at Wiawaka in the summer as a cook. Rachel had fond memories of the women' camp and had enjoyed helping her mother in the kitchen. She reveled in the

Waconda Lodge where a young girl froze to death.

warm, welcoming environment and enjoyed splashing in the crystal waters.

In the autumn of 1958, Rachel set out to find a better life for herself. Her first stop was her favorite spot - Wiawaka. When she arrived, the complex was already closed for the season. Ironically, the place that held such promise for Rachel brusquely turned her away. She sought refuge on the property in Waconda Lodge.

In the 1970s, workmen found Rachel's mummified body in Waconda's porch attic where she had frozen to death years before.

Those who see shadows behind the shaded kitchen windows would like to think that Rachel and her mom are happily reunited in a place with happy memories.

Another phantom plaguing the Fuller House may be the caretaker of the Crosbyside Hotel that once stood on the site where the Rose Cottage now stands.

Before the great hotel burned to the ground in 1905, noted Adirondack photographer Seneca Ray Stoddard likened the Crosbyside to "a great home to which familiar faces come year after year."

This quote takes on new meaning when one visitor staying in Rose Cottage awoke with a start one night and saw a man's face floating at the foot of his bed.

Author's note: When the Trasks passed away they bequeathed their home in Saratoga Springs, known as "Yaddo," to the community as an artists' retreat. This property is also haunted. A ghost chased writer John Cheever out of his room one day.

An architectural remnant of the Lake Placid Club where the apparition of the founder's wife's rocked in her favorite chair.

LAKE PLACID CLUB

Lake Placid owes much of its growth and reputation to Dr. Melvil Dewey, the father of modern library science and founder of the Lake Placid Club.

Starting in his youth, Dewey preached the evils of wasting time. As a student at Amherst, he abhorred the alphabetical arrangement of books because the search for titles took up so much time. His lifelong belief led him to develop a method for classifying books that bears his name – the Dewey Decimal System.

Dewey served as librarian of Columbia University and the State of New York as well as the secretary of the State Board of Regents. Suffering with hay fever, Dewey and his wife settled in Lake Placid for health reasons. They purchased five acres on the east side of Mirror Lake and in 1891, established the Lake Placid Club *the* social and recreational club that initially attracted professors, teachers, clergy, writers, librarians, and ultimately, people of means.

Early days at the exclusive establishment were a financial struggle, but eventually the club's land holdings expanded to over 9,600 acres covering a vast area that extended from Lake Placid Village, beyond the Olympic ski jumps, to the High Peaks wilderness area on Route 73. (The word "loj," as in "Adirondack Loj" is an example of Dewey's philosophy of simplified spelling.)

By 1923, the elite club employed over 1,100, boasted 356 buildings, including a dairy, poultry farms, lecture hall, 21 tennis courts and 7 golf courses.

During the Depression and the years that followed, the Lake Placid Club declined financially.

In 1931, Dewey died in Lake Placid, Florida, where bafflingly, he had attempted to replicate Lake Placid in the Sunshine State.

Dewey and his club were responsible for bringing winter sports to Lake Placid. His son Godfrey carried on the club and was president of the 1932 Lake Placid Winter Olympic Committee. He is credited with single handedly making the Winter Games happen in the resort town, although the expense of hosting the Olympics did little to boost the failing establishment.

During World War II, the U. S. Army operated a reconditioning facility at the onerous resort and accomplished much-needed repair.

While reparations were being made, something unusual occurred at the Lake Placid Club. It seems that all the activity woke up the spirit of Dewey's wife for her apparition appeared in the library (of course) and was seen serenely rocking back and forth in her favorite rocking chair.

STAGECOACH INN

American Indian art, floor to ceiling wainscoting and yellow birch trimmed balcony, fireplaces, and staircase qualify the Stagecoach Inn as quintessentially Adirondack.

The Stagecoach Inn has been serving the public on Old Military Road in Lake Placid since 1833. Some of the inn's more noteworthy guests have been Verplank Colvin, Seneca Ray Stoddard, and William Henry Dana author of *Two Years Before the Mast*, to name just a few.

The ancient structure's dormers, full-length porch bedecked with rocking chairs, and antique weathervane perched on top, provide the perfect backdrop for eerie happenings.

Lodge employees have shared that guests have seen spirits while other visitors merely sense an otherworldly presence. The housekeeping staff has reported that someone, or *something*, steals pillowcases.

In fact, it seems this phantom has a penchant for pillows. At one time, hand crafted pillows with a stagecoach appliqué and the words "Welcome Friends" were carefully placed on the couch as a cherry greeting. Moments later, they were found upside down or turned around even though no *living* soul had been in the room.

Clearly, the invisible presence wasn't in the mood for company that day.

The Stagecoach Inn - home to an overly sensitive spirit.

OLD FORGE HARDWARE

As a child in Lithuania in the 1880s, Moses Cohen regularly accompanied his father to a community thirty miles away to buy poultry, eggs, and grain that they would bring back to sell to the local villagers. Moses learned early on the values of honesty and fair dealing.

When he came to America in 1890, he was only sixteen years old and started his new life as a peddler merchant in the Adirondack Mountains. His pack weighed anywhere from 80 to 100 pounds and was filled with tinware, clothing, and sewing notions. Moses' sales route ran along the Saranac River and took three weeks to walk. Lodging and food cost him fifty cents a night and when he slept in barns during the winter he used blankets from his pack to keep warm.

After two years he had saved enough money to buy a horse and cart. Two years later he partnered with his brother David and bought a hardware store in Bloomingdale, New York. David bought out his brother's interest in 1900; Moses and his wife set out on their own settling in beautiful Old Forge.

Moses started his business from two rented rooms. By this time, the Adirondacks were burgeoning with visitors. The railroad was bringing thousands of wealthy travelers to Old Forge where they would embark on steamships to the many resort hotels, such as the Forge

House, Van Auken's Hotel, and the "Great Camps" owned by Vanderbilt and Morgan. Moses *walked* to the camps for orders - from Old Forge to Inlet, and in the spring, from Eagle Bay to Big Moose.

With the money he saved, Moses was soon able to purchase corner property and have Old Forge Hardware and Furnishings Company constructed.

The lumber industry was flourishing in the Old Forge region due to increased building demands, and business at the hardware store was brisk.

In 1922, an adjacent pool hall caught fire and the raging blaze spread to the store. The loss was devastating, but Moses doggedly rebuilt.

Moses went on to become one of the founders of the first bank in Old Forge and the Adirondack Museum in Blue Mountain Lake. Together with his son they helped established a ski center in Old Forge and built the Forge Motel, the Enchanted Forest, and Howard Johnson's.

The Old Forge Hardware Store is a famous attraction and has been owned by the Cohen family for over one hundred years.

Moses was a man of true grit who made enormous contributions to the community of Old Forge as well as to its commerce. Is it any wonder that some hardware store employees feel that the man's spirit stays behind and tends to business in his venerable store?

Unexplainable noises in the storeroom are attributed to its founder as well as the rush of icy air palpable in the store from time to time. Staff members say the cold chill is Moses carrying on in ethereal form rushing by to stock an empty shelf.

LYDIA SMITH'S GHOST

Paul Smith's College is named for a legendary man whose famous resort on Lower St. Regis Lake was synonymous with Adirondack hospitality.

Apollos A. (Paul) Smith was born in Milton, Vermont in 1825. His work on Erie Canal boats and love of hunting led him to the Adirondack Mountains. The shrewd Vermonter also saw money in the hills and as early as 1860 realized that the real industry of the region was catering to the summer people.

Smith was an excellent woodsman, hunter, and storyteller. His natural abilities and likeability guided him to establish a rustic camp, for men only, near Loon Lake. In 1858, his clientele encouraged him to build an inn so their wives could meet Paul Smith and also enjoy the great outdoors.

Smith purchased fifty acres on Lower St. Regis Lake and put up a frame building with seventeen rooms known simply as "Paul Smith's;" the renowned innkeeper, and his wife Lydia, afforded his guests a home away from home.

Even though the closest railroad was forty miles away, affluent guests endured the rigors of coach travel through the wilderness to enjoy a backwoods experience of the highest fashion. Society columns regularly reported on the charity balls and lavish soirées held at posh resorts in Newport, Rhode Island *and* Paul Smith's.

Smith courted his wife Lydia by hiking thirty miles through the winter woods. Even though she didn't mix with the guests much, they knew she was an important part of the hotel's success. Lydia did all the cooking and managed the daily operations of the lodge that eventually grew to five hundred rooms.

Smith bought up as much land as he could, especially lake frontage. He sold small real estate parcels to folks so they could set up tents. A summer colony grew at Paul Smith's and the campers, naturally, purchased their supplies from Paul Smith.

At the other end of the social spectrum, Smith re-sold some of his land holdings on Upper St. Regis Lake at tremendous profits. This was the first enclave of exclusive private camps in the Adirondacks.

Paul Smith died in 1912 and his two sons ran the hotel until it burned to the ground in 1930. When the sons passed, the entire estate was bequeathed for the founding of a college in Paul Smith's name. The college that specializes in forestry and hotel management is built on the very site of the original resort.

Lydia Smith was an integral ingredient to the development of the early tourist industry in the Adirondacks. Students at the college claim that on moonlit nights the pioneer woman's ghost can sometimes be seen taking a solitary stroll along the shore of Lower St. Regis Lake the place where she once provided so many the time of their lives.

PLATTSBURGH AIR FORCE BASE

Plattsburgh has been associated with the military for centuries. In colonial days, Lake Champlain was part of the "path of empire" in northern New York and Canada. Americans transported men and supplies via the waterway as did the French and British.

In 1776, one of the premier battles of the American Revolution took place south of Plattsburgh off Valcour Island. The area was also the scene of a major conflict during the War of 1812. After that war, 200 acres were sold to the U.S. government to establish a permanent military presence.

In 1944, the Army turned the property over to the Navy who commenced construction of an air base.

After forty years, the airbase closed its doors in the fall of 1995. Since that time the 5,000-acre site has undergone extensive redevelopment and is now a business park, featured on signs along the Adirondack Northway, and is home to diverse companies that include some of the finest aviation facilities in the U.S.

Hundreds of people reside in renovated base housing; bike paths, a boat launch on Lake Champlain, and athletic fields on what was once Air Force training grounds, enliven the site.

Paranormal phenomena perk up the place as well.

Supernatural vestiges of the old air base include reports of a strange, strobe-type light, cold spots, apparitions of children, and a window that refuses to stay covered by blinds or shades; these are just some of the unusual occurrences.

Alarms are triggered for no apparent reason, typewriters clack away, and the sound of horses haunt the area. A Revolutionary War revenant marches back and forth seemingly still standing guard.

There is an ancient burial ground at the former military site. While patrolling the area, security police, who originally disregarded the existence of ghosts, became believers when they witnessed spectral soldiers wandering through the cemetery.

According to a former base employee, the finance building, housed in the old stone barracks, once served as a surgical hospital. Security dogs refused to go into the basement of this building. (People say the walls are painted red to hide the bloodstains!) Supposedly many of the patients confined to bed perished in a fire there and people have reported hearing their screams.

For decades the apparition of a woman in white has spooked the woods surrounding the base.

SACANDAGA VALLEY

Great Sacandaga Lake is the second-largest lake within the Adirondack Park and is actually a reservoir resulting from the damming of the Sacandaga River in 1930. The reservoir was created in an effort to tame the mighty Hudson River and prevent flash flooding and the epidemics that followed in its wake.

At twenty-nine miles long by a maximum of six miles wide, it is a close runner-up to Lake George in size, but lags behind significantly in that the mountains that surround Sacandaga Lake are smaller.

One thing for which it does rival Lake George is boat traffic, as the wide-open expanses of water attract a big display of powerboats, sailboats and jet skis on any given summer weekend.

In simpler times, folks everywhere, but particularly in mountain regions, entertained themselves by telling stories - real or made up. Ghosts have always been fair game when it comes to sharing a good yarn and the Sacandaga Valley certainly has its share of spirits and their tales.

When legislation was passed to build the dam at Conklingville the ramifications swelled far beyond preventing flooding.

Demolition crews were responsible for clearing the forty-two square mile valley; 27,000 acres of homes, businesses, churches, schools, theaters, farms, bridges, and parks had to be vacated before the water rose and swamped fifteen villages.

Even the dead needed to be evacuated. Some claim that not all the buried bodies were moved to higher ground - it was impossible to know where those buried at home were interred. Since coffin parts surfaced and were seen floating in the reservoir, witnesses attest that the disturbed spirits followed and still drift over the lake.

Don Bowman was 17 years old and performed several jobs as a member of the clearing teams in 1927. As he worked alongside the men he closely listened to their stories and carefully recorded the tales. *The Witch of Mad Dog Hill* (skillfully edited by the late Vaughn Ward) is his collection of the supernatural stories he captured as a young man.

My personal favorite is the one about river driver Dutch Jake from Frog Town.

Jake's was a dangerous job ensuring the logs sailed smoothly down river without jamming. Unfortunately he had a mishap and drowned.

The man's habit was to always wear *two* sets of long johns, but when the time came to be buried, his wife dressed him with only one pair.

Night after night his sprit showed up in her bedroom and scared the wits out of her. Finally she moved to get away from his spook but that didn't foil him; Jake showed up in her new digs. She moved once again but it still didn't work - Jake appeared as plain as day alongside her bed.

Out of desperation she visited a "granny woman" for advice. The witch advised that the wife ask Jake what he wanted - why did he keep on haunting her?

That very night when Jake appeared the nervous woman asked him, "What did he want?"

What Jake wanted was another pair of drawers.

The next day, Jake's wife and the witch took a second pair of long johns to his gravesite, dug a little trench for the underwear and buried them.

Jake was never seen again.

Another of Bowman's salvaged tales is about a family - a mother, father, and their son, who took refuge in a log cabin during a rainstorm. Their idea was to ask for a night's lodging in the barn, as was the custom for travelers years back, but when they found the house deserted they made themselves at home.

The man started a fire in the kitchen fireplace and gathered water in buckets from a nearby spring. The woman lit the oil lamp on the kitchen table and cleaned the place up; everything was covered with dust and looked like it had been vacant for quite some time.

They enjoyed a meal of cooked beans, cornbread and water and soon after the father and son retired to the bedroom where they slept in their clothes on cornhusk mattresses.

The mother stayed up for awhile and sat at the table reading her Bible in the light of the kerosene lamp. As she was reading a drop of red liquid fell on to the page. . At first she thought it was pitch from an overhead log, but when a second and third drop appeared, she felt it and smelled it and knew it was blood.

Fearing it was an injured bird or animal she looked up and there sat a man on the edge of the loft his neck slashed from ear to ear.

He said to her, "You're the first person who didn't scream and run away when you saw me. I was murdered by thieves and buried under the floorboards. If you do me a favor and buried my remains under the apple tree you can have all my money that is hidden under the stone next to the tree. The robbers never found it." The man then suddenly disappeared.

The woman ran to tell her husband and showed him the bloodstained page. He believed her because he knew her to be honest.

The next day the family traveled to town and looked up the constable and the priest and told them about the incident. They all traveled back to the house and sure enough, there under the kitchen floorboards was the skeleton.

They carefully removed the remains and dug a grave under the apple tree for the unknown victim. Under a large rock next to the tree was a bag of gold and silver coins that was given to the family by the sheriff. With no known heirs, the money was rightfully theirs.

PAINE HALL

At the northern end of Lake George along the western shore, far from the bright lights and miniature golf courses of Lake George village, is the tiny community of Silver Bay, best known as the home of the Silver Bay Association, a YMCA summer camp founded in 1904.

At the turn of the 20th century, New York City residents Silas and Mary Paine built a beautiful Victorian "cottage" on an elevated point of land overlooking Lake George. They created lovely formal gardens, a sweeping lawn, and flowerbeds that decorated the front of the property. Stonewalls were erected along the road which remain intact today.

Many outbuildings, small sheds, large barn, carriage house, chicken coop, and an icehouse, were constructed in support of the property. The Paines maintained a large vegetable garden and apple orchard as a source of fresh produce; cows were pastured for milk for the cottagers, and chickens supplied fresh eggs.

Paine built both a farmhouse and a barn but by the time the buildings were completed, he had decided that farming would not be practical on the land. He kept the farmhouse for guests and converted the barn into a large house with many bedrooms.

Silas and Mary loved to entertain and there was a constant flow of visitors to Paine Hall. The couple

Paine Hall - a place of history…and mystery.

owned a beautiful launch that they named "Oneita;" the boat was large enough to carry 25 people

In 1901, Thornton Penfield traveled to the Paine property with a group of YMCA secretaries who were responding to Silas' offer to turn his hotel over to the organization to be operated as a Christian conference center.

In 1921, Silas Paine died after a long illness, leaving Mary Paine with the Silver Bay house and estate. She continued to summer there, entertaining often and inviting old friends to stay with her.

Mary died in 1937 and left the estate to Princeton University in memory of their only son, Harrison Spear Paine, who predeceased his parents in 1918.

No one can elaborate on the supernatural at the Christian resort, but several employees have shared that indeed Paine Hall is a mysterious place. Lots of things happen within its walls; "things move around" when no one is in there to move them.

Enough statements have been garnered from Silver Bay staff to conclude that Paine Hall is haunted but unfortunately few specifics can be ascertained. Guests and employees have reported hearing strange noises, and nobody wants to be alone in the house at night.

Is it a Paine family member who lingers here? Does Mrs. Paine carry on alone in the place that she loved? Maybe it's a long-ago guest who refuses to leave.

Although unexplainable events have occurred, no one can say exactly who or what they are, and when and why they happen.

Perhaps that is how it should be at this spiritual place - for the spirit world defies explanation.

ST. REGIS FALLS

One of the spookiest tales to come out of the North Woods involves two men who owned a hunting camp together near St. Regis Falls.

Every season the partners looked forward to a few days of stalking game and each other's company.

After one trip however, Morgan came out of the woods alone. He said that his friend had gotten lost.

Immediately a search party was organized but soon the search for the missing man had to be called off because of blizzard like conditions.

No way did the authorities believe Morgan. They felt by his demeanor that he was guilty but they held no proof. The disappearance was ruled death by accident.

In the spring, the missing man's body was found alongside his rusted rifle. His knife sheath was empty but no one noticed the empty holder lying on the dirt.

Autumn came 'round again and this time Morgan went into the woods with a new friend. After a day in the mountain air, Morgan's companion fell fast asleep but was wide awake when he heard Morgan crying out "Don't do it, don't do it."

The friend lit the lantern and saw Morgan sitting in a chair covered in blood with a knife in his chest. The strange thing is the only fingerprints found on the knife belonged to Morgan's previously deceased partner.

MERRILL MAGEE HOUSE

Warrensburg is known as the "Antique Capital of the Adirondacks" and is the cosmopolitan divide between civilization and the woods. North Country folks exist amidst elegant bed and breakfast inns and restaurants, honky-tonk taverns and quaint shops.

In the early 19th century, Warrensburg was a hub of logging operations due to its location near the confluence of the Hudson and Schroon rivers.

James Warren, who most agree the town was named after, arrived in 1804 and established a tavern and a general store. Unfortunately, Warren drowned seven years later when his skiff overturned on the Hudson.

Another prominent early settler was Stephen Griffin II (1812 - 1893) a well-known lumberman and mill owner. In 1880 he built a tannery in Hamilton County near the town of Wells and eventually a town named Griffin grew up around the mill - now a ghost town.

In 1875 he was a member of the state legislature and twice held the office of town supervisor. Warrensburg remembers him warmly as a compassionate individual

Stephen Griffin II was named for his grandfather who served in the Army during the American Revolution. Grandfather Griffin was stationed at Valley Forge during the brutal winter of 1780 and also guarded Joshua Smith the man who arranged the secret meeting between traitor Benedict Arnold and Major John André.

The Merrill Magee - where the former lady of the house still roams.

In 1981 the Carrington family purchased the estate of Grace Merrill Magee. They set about converting the private home into a traditional country inn. Grace, who was the longest resident of the house, took after her mother in that she was devoted to maintaining the house and gardens as her grandfather, Stephen Griffin II, had left them.

The Merrill Magee house is steeped in the history of our nation's past and plays a large part in Warrensburg's history. The home is meticulously maintained and takes great pride in its place on the National Register of Historic Places.

The tavern and reception rooms are the original structure purchased in 1839. The Greek Revival façade was added in the 1850s, and in the 1920s, Grace added the back section, the current large dining room. Grace was also responsible for installing the 1928 swimming pool supposedly the oldest private pool in New York.

Today you'll find the graciousness of an earlier era at the bed and breakfast inn. You may even feel the presence of the former lady of the house who some say still roams the environs. On occasion, a door will open and close of its own accord as if someone has just come through.

Once a Carrington son spied a specter peering out an upstairs window and at times, whisperings of disembodied voices are heard in this same room.

The Merrill Magee House is not your typical haunted house but reminiscent of any historic home where owners rejoice in preserving the past. The subtle footsteps heard upstairs are gentle reminders of one who once lived there.

A female wraith occupies the Wait House now home to a women's social service agency.

ACKNOWLEDGEMENTS

I want to recognize Anne LaBastille, Ph.D. (a.k.a. *Woodswoman*) for her inspiration and encouragement.

I also want to convey sincere thanks to the following individuals for their assistance in obtaining information for this book:

Mary Baer
Sue Baer
Jerry Bearden
S. Lee Bowden
Lisa & Will Carpenter
Amil Droz
Sally Erskine
Tricia Hayes
Judy Johnson
Mary Mackenzie

Shirley McFerson
Muriel Morrison
Beverly O'Neill
Kelley Oram
Doris H. Patton
Beverly P. Reid
Kelly Street
Patricia Steele
Marilyn Van Dyke, Ph.D.
Lyn Witte

Special thanks to my North Woods distributor Rob Igoe and the staff of North Country Books.

BIBLIOGRAPHY

Aber, Ted, *Adirondack Folks.* North Country Books, Utica, NY; 1980.

Bowman, Don, *The Witch of Mad Dog Hill.* Bowman Books, The Greenfield Review Press, Greenfield Center, NY; 1999.

"A Ghostly Fish Story." *The Sentinel* (undated).

Gosselink, Charles G., *Benjamin Van Buren's Bay.* Boathouse Books, Silver Bay, NY; 2002.

"Halloween: The Perfect Time To Tell Ghost Stories." *Adirondack Express*, Old Forge, NY; October 24, 1995.

Hauck, Dennis William, *Haunted Places, The National Directory.* Penguin Books, New York, NY; 1996.

Jones, Louis, Ph.D., *Things That Go Bump in the Night.* Syracuse University Press, Syracuse, NY; 1959 and 1983.

Leonbruno, Frank, *Lake George Reflections.* Purple Mountain Press, Ltd., Fleischmanns, NY; 1998.

Little, Gordon, "Ghost story of old stands up to test of time." *Press Republican*, Plattsburgh, NY; August 12, 2001.

Marvel, Janet, "The Maranvilles, A century of Bolton transportation." *The Chronicle*, Glens Falls, NY; August 19-23, 1993.

O'Brien, Kathryn E., *The Great and the Gracious on Millionaires' Row.* North Country Books, Utica, NY; 1978.

Pitkin, David J., *Ghosts of the Northeast.* Aurora Publications, Salem, NY; 2002.

Shaw, Christopher, "Died and Gone To Your House," *Adirondack Life.* Jay, NY; November/December 1987.

Satterlee, Sheila, "Tratelja." *The Lake George Mirror* (undated).

Seay, Suzanne, "Otherworld." *The Post Star,* Glens Falls, NY; October 27, 1996.

"The Tinware Peddler," Town of Webb Historical Association News, Fall 2001.

Tolnay, Thomas, *Spirits of the Adirondacks.* Birch Bark Press, Delphi, NY; 2001.

White, William Chapman, *Adirondack Country.* Alfred A. Knopf, Inc., New York, NY; 1954.

WEBSITES

Ausable Chasm: ausablechasm.com
The Haunted North Country: apnmag.com
The History of Major Robert Rogers: reangerring.com
Lake George History: lakegeorge-ny.com
Landon Hill Bed & Breakfast: bedandbreakfast.net
The Merrill Magee House: merrillmageehouse.com
Plattsburgh Airbase Redevelopment Corporation: parc-usa.com
Plattsburgh AFB and the 380 BW: phil123.addr.com
Sabael Benedict: avenet.org/ne-do-ba
Sagamore History: thesagamore.com

Look for these other titles by

Lynda Lee Macken

ADIRONDACK GHOSTS

GHOSTLY GOTHAM – NEW YORK CITY'S
HAUNTED HISTORY

HAUNTED HISTORY OF STATEN ISLAND

HAUNTED SALEM & BEYOND

GHOSTS OF THE GARDEN STATE

HAUNTED CAPE MAY

GHOSTS OF THE GARDEN STATE II

or contact:

BLACK CAT PRESS
Post Office Box 1218
Forked River, New Jersey 08731

llmacken@hotmail.com